Helping Children See Jesus

ISBN: 978-1-64104-047-1

THE CRUCIFIXION PART 2
Christ's Sacrifice, Our Salvation
New Testament Volume 12: Life of Christ Part 12

Author: Ruth B. Greiner
Illustrator: Frances H. Hertzler
Computer Graphic Artist: Ed Olson
Typesetting and Layout: Patricia Pope

© 2018 Bible Visuals International
PO Box 153, Akron, PA 17501-0153
Phone: (717) 859-1131
www.biblevisuals.org

All rights reserved. No part of this publication may be reproduced, stored in a retrieval system or transmitted in any form by any means, electronic, mechanical, photocopy, recording or otherwise, without the prior permission of the publisher, except as provided by USA copyright law.

RELATED ITEMS

To access related items (such as activities, memory verse posters and translated texts) please visit our web store at shop.biblevisuals.org and enter 1012 in the search box on the page.

FREE TEXT DOWNLOAD

To access a FREE printable copy of the teaching text (PDF format) in English or other available languages, enter S1012DL in the search box. Add the item to your cart, and use coupon code XTACSV17 at checkout. Once your order is processed you will receive an email with a link to the free download.

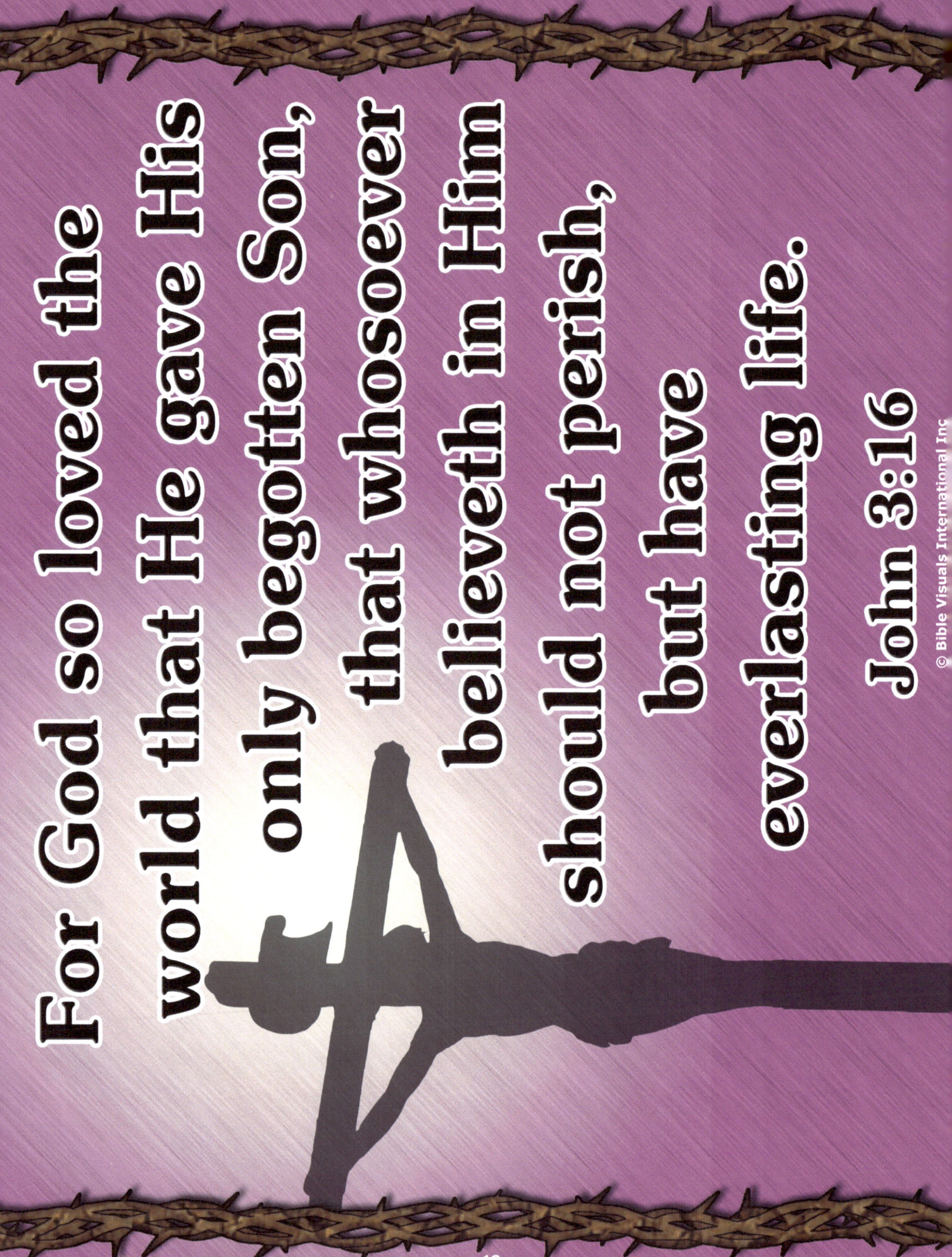

Lesson 1
JESUS DENIED AND ACCUSED

Scripture to be studied: Matthew 26:57-75; Mark 14:53-72; Luke 22:54-71; John 18:12-27.

The *aim* of the lesson: To show that though Christians may determine to do right, sometimes they fail.

What your students should *know*: Jesus loves them even if they do wrong. He is willing to forgive them if they confess their sin.

What your students should *feel*: The need of forgiveness when they sin.

What your students should *do*: Ask the Lord Jesus to forgive their sin. Tell Him they love Him.

Lesson outline (for the teacher's and students' notebooks):
1. The disciples forsake Jesus (John 18:12-24).
2. Jesus is taken to the rulers and falsely accused (Matthew 26:57-68; Mark 14:53-65).
3. Peter denies Christ three times (Matthew 26:69-74; Mark 14:66-72; Luke 22:54-60; John 18:25-27).
4. The Lord Jesus continues to love Peter (Matthew 26:75; Mark 14:72; Luke 22:61-62).

The verse to be memorized:

For God so loved the world, that He gave His only begotten Son, that whosoever believeth in Him should not perish, but have everlasting life. (John 3:16)

NOTE TO THE TEACHER

Again (as in the previous volume) we see certain prophetic Scriptures fulfilled in the events leading up to and including the crucifixion of our Lord Jesus Christ. In this first lesson:

The disciples of Christ forsake Him (Zechariah 13:7).

Peter, one of His closest disciples, denies Christ three times as prophesied by the Lord Himself (Matthew 26:34; Mark 14:30; Luke 22:34; John 13:38).

Jesus remains silent when the witnesses lie about Him (Isaiah 53:7).

His enemies hit Him and spit on Him (Isaiah 50:6).

According to the plan of God, the Lord Jesus was to die for the sin of the world. Nothing could keep Him from accomplishing this purpose.

You will want to stress this truth: it is possible for a believer to determine to do what is right (as Peter had done), and to fail (as Peter did). As the Lord Jesus prayed for Peter, so He prays for us: that our faith will not fail; that if we sin, we will return to Him (Luke 22:31-32).

THE LESSON
1. THE DISCIPLES FORSAKE JESUS
John 18:12-24

Peter was running! James and John were running! Nathanael and the other disciples were running! They were running from the Garden of Gethsemane, leaving Jesus alone with the soldiers who had bound Him. Peter and his companions were afraid. What awful things would happen next?

Only a few hours before Peter had promised Jesus, "I will never desert You, even if all the others run away. I will lay down my life for You. I will not deny You." Yet at this very moment Peter was deserting Jesus. He was running away. How could he have forgotten his promise so quickly? How could he and the other disciples leave Jesus alone in the hands of His enemies?

Troubled thoughts were filling Peter's mind: *Where will they take Jesus? What will they do to Him? Surely Jesus understands that if I had stayed with Him I would have been captured, too.* Peter knew he should not be running away. Suddenly he stopped. He determined to return and follow Jesus–but at a safe distance.

Another disciple, John, decided to turn back with Peter. Through the dark night they followed the mob as they led Jesus from the garden. They took Him to Annas who was waiting. (Annas, the father-in-law of Caiaphas the high priest, had once been the high priest, so he still held some authority.) It was to Annas that the officers first led Jesus.

John, who knew Annas, entered the courtyard with the officers. But Peter had to wait outside until John convinced a maid to let Peter in. It was a cool night and the servants and officers gathered about the fire to warm themselves.

Show Illustration #1

Quietly Peter joined them. The maid who had let Peter in watched him closely. At last she asked, "Are you also a disciple of that Man?" She was referring of course to the Lord Jesus.

"I am not!" Peter answered quickly.

At that same time Jesus was being questioned by Annas in a room alongside the courtyard. The questions were about His disciples and His teachings.

Jesus answered, "What I have taught is well known. I preached in the synagogue and in the temple. Some of the Jewish leaders who heard Me are here. Ask them what I said."

One of the officers standing nearby slapped Jesus. "Is that the way to answer the high priest?" he demanded.

Jesus answered, "If I have said something wrong, tell Me of it. But if I have spoken the truth, why did you strike Me?"

No one could answer. No one could think of one wrong thing Jesus had said or done. He had done only what was right.

Annas had no more questions for Jesus. "Take Him to Caiaphas," he ordered.

2. JESUS IS TAKEN TO THE RULERS AND FALSELY ACCUSED
Matthew 26:57-68; Mark 14:53-65

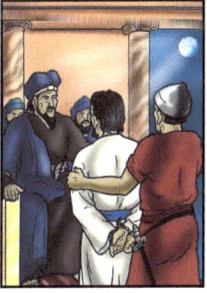

Show Illustration #2

Then Jesus, His hands tied tightly behind Him, was led to the house of Caiaphas (probably located on another side of the courtyard). Caiaphas was the high priest of God. He was to speak to God for men. He was also to speak to men for God. But he was sinful. He did not accept the Lord Jesus as the Messiah of Israel, the Son of God.

Caiaphas was not alone in his room. The Sanhedrin, a council of 70 judges, had met with him. The chief priests were there too. They had been busy searching out

– 19 –

men who would speak against Jesus. The witnesses were brought forward to testify. One witness told of something which, he said, he had heard Jesus say. Another witness reported something else. Still another told a different story. But none of the witnesses said the same thing. According to the Jewish law no man could be condemned unless at least two people testified exactly alike. Why did the witnesses not agree? Because they were telling lies.

Then two more witnesses said: "We heard Him say, 'I will destroy this temple that is made with hands, and in three days I will build another made without hands.'" What Jesus had really said was: "Destroy this temple [My body] (See John 2:21.) and in three days I will raise it up" (John 2:19). But even these two witnesses did not agree perfectly in their testimonies. (See Mark 14:59.)

When the witnesses finished speaking, Caiaphas turned to Jesus and asked, "Have You no answer to all these charges against You?"

But Jesus did not answer.

The high priest spoke again: "I command You by the living God to tell us: Are you the Christ, the Son of God?"

Jesus said, "I am."

Angrily the high priest tore his clothes. He shouted, "We do not need any other witnesses! You have all heard the blasphemy! What do you say?" (Blasphemy is claiming to be God or speaking against God.)

"He is guilty! He deserves to die!" they all shouted.

Some spit in Jesus' face. Others slapped His face. One put a blindfold on Him while another slapped Him. "Tell us now who hit You, if You are really a prophet!" they shouted. Laughingly they mocked Him.

But Jesus did not strike back. He did not stop the men from hurting Him. He did not hate those who hated Him. He knew His time to suffer had come.

3. PETER DENIES CHRIST THREE TIMES
Matthew 26:69-74; Mark 14:66-72; Luke 22:54-60; John 18:25-27

Peter, meanwhile, slipped quietly away from the fire and to the porch which led out to the street. While he waited there expecting to learn what would happen to Jesus, he heard a rooster crow. Instantly he should have remembered Jesus' warning that before the rooster crowed twice, he would deny the Son of God three times. But Peter did not remember. Instead of repenting and getting closer to Jesus, Peter seemed to get farther away.

Another maid who saw Peter turned to some of the men, saying, "This man also was with Jesus."

Show Illustration #3

"I do not even know Him!" Peter shouted with a curse.

A man standing nearby said, "But you *are* one of them."

"I am not!" Peter roared.

About an hour later another man glared knowingly at Peter. He was a servant of the high priest and a relative of Malchus (whose ear Peter had cut off). "Did I not see you in the garden with Him?" he asked. "I am sure you were with Him. You talk like a Galilean."

Again Peter cursed. "I do not know what you are talking about," he sneered. "I do not know that Man!" While Peter was still talking, he heard the rooster crow a second time.

4. THE LORD JESUS CONTINUES TO LOVE PETER
Matthew 26:75; Mark 14:72; Luke 22:61-62

Show Illustration #4

At that very moment Peter saw Jesus looking at him. It was a sad look, but a loving look. Peter then remembered Jesus' words: "Before the rooster crows twice, you will deny Me three times." It had happened exactly as Jesus said it would, though Peter had insisted he would never deny his Lord.

Immediately Peter ran away to a quiet place where he could be alone. There he wept bitterly.

Peter had learned a hard lesson. In his own strength he could not do what was right. In his weakness he had failed the Lord Jesus. He truly loved the Lord. Now he had sworn, declaring he never even knew Him. Yet, in spite of his great sin, Jesus loved him.

Like Peter, we are weak. At times we grieve the Lord Jesus by the things we say and do. Yet Jesus loves us and is willing to answer our prayer for forgiveness. (See 1 John 1:9.) Have you asked Him to forgive your sin? Have you thanked Him for His love?

Lesson 2
THE TRIALS

Scripture to be studied: Matthew 27:1-31; Mark 15:1-20; Luke 23:1-25; John 18:28-40; 19:1-16

The *aim* of the lesson: To show that in His sufferings, Jesus obediently did the will of God.

What your students should *know*: Jesus endured the lies and mocking because of His love for sinners.

What your students should *feel*: Grateful for the love of Jesus.

What your students should *do*: Thank Him for suffering for them.

Lesson outline (for the teacher's and students' notebooks):
1. Jesus is taken to Pilate and Judas realizes he has sinned (Matthew 27:1-10; Mark 15:1; Luke 23:1; John 18:28).
2. Jesus is accused before Pilate (Matthew 27:11-14; Mark 15:2-5; Luke 23:2-5; John 18:28-38).
3. Herod mocks Jesus (Luke 23:6-12).
4. Jesus is sentenced to death (Matthew 27:15-26; Mark 15:6-15; Luke 23:13-25; John 18:38-40; 19:1-16).

The verse to be memorized:

For God so loved the world, that He gave His only begotten Son, that whosoever believeth in Him should not perish, but have everlasting life. (John 3:16)

NOTE TO THE TEACHER

Before teaching this lesson, we who handle the Word of God should take account of ourselves. Peter knew that his only hope for eternity was in the Lord Jesus. Until this night he apparently did not realize that his *daily life* had to be controlled by the Lord Jesus. His noble purposes ended in failure. The steps which led to his failure were:

1. Peter was self-confident. He trusted in himself. (Study Luke 22:31-34.)
2. Peter was careless about prayer. Peter had boasted that he was ready to die with the Lord Jesus. Only a short time later he fell asleep when he should have been praying. (Study Mark 14:27-38.)
3. Peter failed to seek the will of his Lord. (See Luke 22:49-50.) When Judas betrayed Jesus, the disciples asked if they should use their swords in defense. Instead of waiting for His answer, Peter used his sword to cut off the right ear of the servant.
4. Peter followed afar off. (See Luke 22:54.) Peter was far from the One he had promised to die for because he fell asleep and did not pray.
5. Peter warmed himself at the fire of the enemy. (See Luke 22:55.) He was with those who hated Christ!
6. Peter resumed the practice of an old habit. (Study Mark 14:71.) As a fisherman, Peter doubtless swore frequently. But that habit had been put away three years before when he turned from fishing to following the Saviour.
7. Peter denied his Lord. (See Luke 22:57-60.) Others might deny Christ, Peter had said; he *never* would. But he did!*

If we are to be fruitful in our ministry, we must recognize that we are weak. When our dependence is in the Lord alone, we shall be useful in His service. Remember, as Jesus prayed for Peter, so He prays for you (Hebrews 7:25).

From *The Life and Letters of Saint Peter* by E. Schuyler English (Loizeaux Brothers).

Because of its sadness, it is difficult to teach about the suffering of our Lord. Yet His suffering was necessary for our salvation. And it perfectly fulfilled prophetic Scripture.

In this lesson Christ is before Pilate and Herod. He was subjected to mockery and ridicule because He chose to do the will of God. We can never understand the love which compelled the Lord Jesus to endure such suffering. May God give you special wisdom in presenting this lesson.

THE LESSON

Pilate, the governor of Judea, had come to Jerusalem at the time of the Passover. He had not come to take part in the Passover feast, for he was not a Jew. He was a Roman sent to keep law and order in this land which had been conquered by Rome.

As a new governor in Judea, Pilate was eager to keep peace among the Jews. He wanted Caesar, the emperor of Rome, to hear that he, Pilate, was a good governor who was ruling the people well.

1. JESUS IS TAKEN TO PILATE AND JUDAS REALIZES HE HAS SINNED
Matthew 27:1-10; Mark 15:1; Luke 23:1; John 18:28

But all was not well in Jerusalem. Jesus Christ had been taken prisoner and the Jewish leaders claimed He was guilty of death. Caiaphas, the high priest, and the Sanhedrin (a council of 70 judges) had condemned Him. But they did not have the authority to put Him to death since the Romans were ruling the land. It seemed that Pilate had arrived in Jerusalem at exactly the right time to sentence Christ.

Show Illustration #5

It was early morning when the chief priests and scribes led Jesus, bound, to the royal palace. These men hoped Pilate would quickly sentence Him to death.

Outside the palace, on the streets of Jerusalem, walked a lonely, miserable man: Judas. He had betrayed Jesus for 30 pieces of silver. The sound of the silver jingling in his money bag haunted Judas. He had learned what happened after he betrayed Jesus: Jesus had been ridiculed and condemned by Caiaphas and the council. Jesus was now on trial before Pilate. Judas knew he had done a terrible deed. But what could he do to change it? He could have confessed his sin and prayed to God for forgiveness. Instead, he hurried to the temple. There he found the chief priests who had paid him to betray Jesus. "I have sinned for I betrayed innocent blood," he said.

"What does that matter to us?" the chief priests answered carelessly.

Judas threw the silver coins on the floor. Then he turned, left the temple, went out–and hanged himself!

The chief priests picked up the silver pieces which had scattered on the temple floor. "What shall we do with this money?" one asked. "It is against our law to put the money into our collection, for it is the price of blood."

Discussing the matter further, they decided to use the money to buy a nearby field in which to bury foreigners. After the priests bought the field, it became known as the Field of Blood.

2. JESUS IS ACCUSED BEFORE PILATE
Matthew 27:11-14; Mark 15:2-5; Luke 23:2-5; John 18:28-38

Meanwhile, inside the palace Jesus stood on trial before Pilate. Pilate wondered what wrong the prisoner had done.

Show Illustration #6

He went outside where the chief priests and others waited. "What charge do you bring against this Man?" Pilate asked.

"If He were not an evil-doer we would not have brought Him to you," they shouted.

Pilate said, "Take Him yourselves and judge Him according to your law."

The Jews answered, "It is against our law for us to put anyone to death."

Someone called out, "This Man caused trouble in our nation."

Another added falsely, "He tells us we should not pay taxes to Caesar."

Others cried out, "He claims He is Christ our King!"

Pilate, after hearing these accusations, went back into the palace to talk to Jesus. "Are You the King of the Jews?" he asked.

Jesus answered, "You have said it, for I am a King. That is why I was born and why I came into the world. I came to bring truth."

The things Jesus said troubled Pilate. But he could find no reason to put Jesus to death. So he went out to the chief priests and crowds and told them, "I find no fault in this Man."

Angrily, the chief priests shouted many things which they said Jesus had done. Finally Pilate turned to Jesus asking, "Do you hear how much they are saying against You?"

Jesus stood strong–and silent. He could have honestly told Pilate that the accusations were lies. But He did not.

"Are you going to answer?" Pilate demanded. Jesus did not say one word.

The people shouted their hatred. "His teaching has stirred up men and women throughout all of Judea and Galilee."

3. HEROD MOCKS JESUS
Luke 23:6-12

When Pilate learned that Jesus was a Galilean, he sent Him to Herod, the Roman ruler of Galilee. Herod was visiting in Jerusalem at that time. Although Herod and Pilate were not friends, Pilate thought this was a good way to avoid passing sentence on Jesus.

Herod was glad that Pilate sent the prisoner to him. He had heard many things about Jesus and for a long time wanted to see Him. Perhaps Jesus would do a miracle for him.

But King Herod was disappointed. Jesus did not answer one of his questions. Even though the chief priests and scribes (who went along with Jesus) accused Him again and again, Jesus stood silent. (See Isaiah 53:7.)

Herod then decided that if he could not get Jesus to speak or do a miracle, he and his soldiers would make fun of Him.

Show Illustration #7

They began to mock and scoff at the Son of God. They dressed Him in a royal robe. For a scepter they gave Him a reed. Finally they sent Him back to Pilate.

4. JESUS IS SENTENCED TO DEATH
Matthew 27:15-26; Mark 15:6-15;
Luke 23:13-25; John 18:38-40; 19:1-16

What was Pilate to do? He called the chief priests and the rulers and the people together. "You brought this Man to me as One who has caused trouble," he declared. "I have examined Him and–like Herod–I find no fault in Him. This Man has done nothing worthy of death."

Pilate knew he should let Jesus go. But he wanted to keep peace among the people of Judea. Even more important, he wanted to please Caesar. Pilate asked himself, *How can I get out of all this?* Then he had an idea. Turning to the people, he said, "You have a custom that one prisoner may be released at Passover time. Do you want me to release this prisoner–the King of the Jews? Or shall I release the murderer, Barabbas?"

The people shouted, "We want Barabbas, not Jesus! Release Barabbas!"

As the crowds shouted, the wife of Pilate came to him. "Have nothing to do with this righteous Man," she pleaded. "I was very troubled last night in my dreams about Him."

Pilate was confused. He turned to the crowds and asked again, "Which of the two shall I release to you–Jesus or Barabbas?"

The people cried, "Away with this Man and release Barabbas!"

Then Pilate gave the orders to have Jesus flailed. Some of his soldiers twisted thorns into a crown. They pressed it on His head. Again they placed the purple robe on His shoulders. "Hail, King of the Jews!" they shouted as they struck Him.

Show Illustration #8

Pilate went out to the crowds. This time he took Jesus with him. "Look!" he called out. "I bring Him to you so you may know I find no crime in Him. What shall I do with Him whom you call the King of the Jews?"

"Crucify Him! Crucify Him!" they screamed.

"Why? What evil has He done?" the Roman governor asked. "I have found no cause of death in Him. I will whip Him and let Him go."

But they cried loudly, "Let Him be crucified!"

Finally Pilate sat down (on the judgment seat, a place called The Pavement). Jesus stood before the angry, shouting mob. Pointing at Jesus, Pilate cried, "Here is your King!"

"Away with Him! Away with Him! Crucify Him!" the crowd shouted.

Pilate asked, "Shall I crucify your King?"

"We have no king but Caesar," they answered.

Pilate realize he couldn't change their minds and asked for a basin of water. He washed his hands in it before the people saying, "I am innocent of the blood of this righteous Man. You see to it."

"We and our children accept responsibility for His death!" the people shrieked.

Then, after having Jesus scourged with a whip, Pilate handed Him over to the people to be crucified. Pilate had washed his hands with water. But he was guilty of sentencing the Son of God to death.

Jesus suffered in your place and mine. Have you thanked Him? If not, will you do so now?

Lesson 3
THE CRUCIFXION

Scripture to be studied: Matthew 27:27-66; Mark 15:16-47; Luke 23:26-56; John 19:16-42

The *aim* of the lesson: To show how Jesus suffered as our sacrifice for sin.

What your students should *know*: Because Jesus died, it is possible for all who place their trust in Him to have forgiveness of sins.

What your students should *feel*: Awe, considering what it cost the Lord Jesus to provide forgiveness of sins.

What your students should *do*: Receive the Lord Jesus as Saviour from sin.

Lesson outline (for the teacher's and students' notebooks):

1. Jesus is crucified and asks God to forgive the soldiers (Matthew 27:27-38; Mark 15:16-28; Luke 23:26-38; John 19:17-24).
2. One thief turns to Jesus and is assured of His forgiveness (Matthew 27:39-44; Mark 15:29-32; Luke 23:39-43; John 19:25-27).
3. Jesus gives Himself to die (Matthew 27:45-54; Mark 15:33-39; Luke 23:44-48; John 19:28-37).
4. Jesus is buried (Matthew 27:55-66; Mark 15:40-47; Luke 23:49-56; John 19:38-42).

The verse to be memorized:

For God so loved the world, that He gave His only begotten Son, that whosoever believeth in Him should not perish, but have everlasting life. (John 3:16)

> **NOTE TO THE TEACHER**
>
> No words or pictures can fully describe all the suffering and agony Jesus bore in our place. In this lesson we see the accurate fulfillment of Genesis 3:15; Isaiah 53:1-12; Psalm 22:1-21; and many other Old Testament Scriptures.
>
> When Jesus cried, "It is finished!" He was referring to the work which God the Father had given Him to do–a work which had been proclaimed by the prophets. Jesus gave His life as the perfect sacrifice for sin, ending the law that required animal sacrifices. Jesus died as our Sacrifice–once and for all. What a wonderful Saviour He is! And what a great salvation He purchased for us!
>
> Teacher, ask God for a fresh and deeper appreciation of His work of grace accomplished at Calvary.

THE LESSON

Jesus was tired. Through the long night and early morning He had stood before His enemies. They had whipped Him with leather straps which tore His flesh. His head was bruised and sore from the crown of thorns. His bound arms ached. Worst of all, His heart was filled with sorrow for the sins of the people who were treating Him cruelly.

Much had happened during the past two days. Judas, one of the disciples, had betrayed Jesus for 30 silver coins. Peter, another disciple, denied three times that he ever knew Jesus. Soldiers had spit in His face and slapped Him. The high priest had accused the Son of God of blasphemy. The crowds had jeered at Him and begged for His death. Herod had mocked Him. Pilate had finally given way to the people and their demands and sentenced Him to death by crucifixion.

Have you ever wondered why Jesus had to suffer so much and why He did it so willingly? He did it because He loves us. Today as you listen, remind yourself, "He did it for *me*."

Barabbas, the murderer, had been set free. Jesus, the perfect One, had been condemned to die on a cross. After Pilate pronounced this dreadful sentence, he had Jesus scourged again.

Then the soldiers took Jesus into the palace where they continued to mock and torment Him. He wore the purple robe they had placed upon Him. The soldiers bowed before Him pretending to worship Him. Then they stood and saluted Him, saying, "Hail, King of the Jews!" But the soldiers did not believe that Jesus was the Son of God nor that He would ever be King–certainly not the King of all kings.

Jesus silently endured the mocking, spitting, slapping, and the whippings. When the soldiers had had their fun, they took the robe off Jesus and put His own clothes back on Him.

1. JESUS IS CRUCIFIED AND ASKS GOD TO FORGIVE THE SOLDIERS
Matthew 27:27-38; Mark 15:16-28; Luke 23:26-38; John 19:17-24

The soldiers led Jesus out of the palace. In view of the crowd they thrust a heavy cross on His shoulder. The weight of the cross caused Jesus and the crowd to move slowly through the narrow city streets. Outside the walls of Jerusalem, Jesus fell beneath His heavy load. So the soldiers ordered a man (named Simon) to carry the cross for Him. Then the procession moved on.

At last they came to the hill of Golgotha (also called Calvary). From a distance the hill looked like a huge skull. This was the customary place for criminals to be put to death.

The people crowded around to watch. A soldier offered Jesus some vinegar mixed with myrrh. By drinking it He would not feel the awful pain which soon would be His. But when Jesus tasted it He refused to drink it. He had to suffer all the pain. (See Psalm 69:21.)

Show Illustration #9

The soldiers ripped the clothes off Jesus and wound a cloth around His loins. Then they made Him lie down upon the cross. With His arms stretched out, they drove spikes through His hands. When the cross was lifted and set in place, a spike was hammered through His feet. On either side of Jesus two thieves were crucified.

It was nine o'clock in the morning when the soldiers completed their dreadful work. Hanging before them Jesus prayed, "Father, forgive them, for they do not know what they are doing."

The soldiers, who seemed not to notice the suffering of Jesus, divided His clothes into four parts, one part for each soldier. Because His outer robe had been woven without a seam, one of the soldiers said, "Instead of tearing it, let us cast lots [dice] for it to decide whose it should be." This they did, thus fulfilling (without their knowing it!) precisely what the Scripture, many years before, had said they would do. (See Psalm 22:18.)

Pilate had instructed that a sign be put on the cross of Jesus, reading, "This is Jesus of Nazareth, the King of the Jews." It was written in three languages: in Hebrew for the Jewish people to read; in Latin for the Roman soldiers to read; and in Greek, the common language in Jerusalem at that time.

2. ONE THIEF TURNS TO JESUS AND IS ASSURED OF FORGIVENESS
Matthew 27:39-44; Mark 15:29-32;
Luke 23:39-43; John 19:25-27

Show Illustration #10

The people who passed by the cross looked up at Jesus, mocking Him. They wagged their heads (Psalm 22:7) and shouted, "You, who can destroy the temple and rebuild it in three days, if You are really the Son of God, come down from the cross!"

Then the chief priests and rulers scoffed, saying, "He saved others, but He cannot save Himself. Let the Christ, the King of Israel, now come down from the cross so we may see and believe. He trusts God; let God deliver Him, for He said, 'I am the Son of God'" (Psalm 22:8). One of the thieves on the cross beside Jesus sneered: " If You are the Christ, save Yourself and us!"

The thief on the other cross answered, "Do you not fear God even when you are getting the same punishment He is? We deserve death. But this Man has done nothing wrong." Then he turned to Jesus saying, "Lord, remember me when You come into Your Kingdom."

Jesus answered, "I tell you this, today you will be with Me in Paradise [a place of joy and comfort]." The thief believed what Jesus said. He believed that Jesus is indeed the Son of God.

Near the cross stood Mary, the mother of Jesus, and her sister. Mary Magdalene (from whom Jesus had cast out demons) was also there. With these women was John, the disciple whom Jesus loved in a special way. They were all filled with great sorrow.

Jesus looked down at His mother. He wanted someone to care for her. He said to her, "Look, there is your son." Then He spoke to John: "Look, she is your mother." From that time on, John took Mary, the mother of Jesus, to his own home to care for her.

3. JESUS GIVES HIMSELF TO DIE
Matthew 27:45-54; Mark 15:33-39;
Luke 23:44-48; John 19:28-37

Show Illustration #11

At twelve o'clock noon, although it was the middle of the day, the sky suddenly grew dark as night. The people were frightened. They could not understand it. They had never seen anything like it. The darkness lasted for one hour . . . two hours . . . three hours.

At three o'clock, Jesus cried with a loud voice, "My God, My God, why have You forsaken Me?" (See Psalm 22:1.) Never, never had God the Father and God the Son been separated. But on the cross the perfect, sinless Lord Jesus became sin for us. He bore all our sins in His body. Sin always separates us from God. Nothing–no suffering of any kind–could be compared to the agonizing suffering of His being separated from His Father, God.

A bit later Jesus said, "I am thirsty." Someone filled a sponge with vinegar, put it on a branch and held it up to His mouth. (Another prophecy about His death was thus fulfilled. See Psalm 69:21.) When Jesus had tasted the vinegar He cried with a loud, strong voice, "It is finished! Father, I commend My spirit into Your hands." (See Psalm 31:5.) Then He bowed His head and by His own choice, gave up His spirit and died.

At that moment there was a great earthquake. Rocks broke and buildings shook. The captain of the Roman soldiers, who had watched Jesus die, exclaimed, "Surely this Man was the Son of God!"

To be certain the three men on the crosses would be dead before the sun went down, Pilate commanded the soldiers to break their legs. First they broke the legs of the two thieves. But when they got to Jesus they saw He was already dead. So they did not break His legs. (Unknown to them, another prophecy was fulfilled. See Psalm 34:20.) One of the soldiers used a spear to pierce the side of Jesus. (See Zechariah 12:10.) And from His side came out blood and water–a sign that when He died His heart was broken. (See Psalm 69:20.)

4. JESUS IS BURIED
Matthew 27:55-66; Mark 15:40-47;
Luke 23:49-56; John 19:38-42

Show Illustration #12

When it was evening a rich man (of Arimathaea) named Joseph went to Pilate and begged him for the body of Jesus. Pilate gave Joseph permission to take the body from the cross. Nicodemus, who had once gone to Jesus at night, helped Joseph. They wrapped His body in a long, clean linen cloth with spices, as was the custom of the Jews. Then they carried it to a nearby garden and placed it inside a new tomb, rolling a great stone in front of the opening.

The agony of the cross was over. Through His death, Jesus made it possible for everyone who would believe on Him to have complete forgiveness of sin.

Have you said, "Thank You, Lord Jesus, for dying for me?" Have you believed Him to be the Son of God? Have you received His offer of salvation which cost Him so much suffering? If you have never placed your trust in Him as your Saviour, will you do so right now?

Lesson 4
THE CRUCIFXION OF OUR LORD

NOTE TO THE TEACHER

As you have studied these lessons in the Bible, you have repeatedly observed this statement: "that the Scriptures might be fulfilled." Hundreds of years before these events took place, God had told precisely what would occur. Depending upon the age of your students, you may wish to discuss Psalm 22:1-21 with its clear account of death by crucifixion:

1. The cry of desertion (v. 1)
2. Darkness (v. 2)
3. Mocking and ridicule (vv. 6-8)
4. The bones out of joint (v. 14)
5. Sweating caused by extreme suffering (v. 14)
6. Weakness and thirst (v. 15)
7. Hands and feet pierced (v. 16)
8. Casting of lots (v. 18)

Other prophecies which could be studied are Psalm 69 (especially verses 4, 7-8, 10-12, 21); Isaiah 50:6; Isaiah 53:3-7, 9-12; and Zechariah 12:10. It should be remembered that although crucifixion was a Roman form of execution, it was perfectly foretold by Jewish prophets.

When Jesus died, the Scriptures were fulfilled. What God said would happen, happened. (See 2 Peter 1:21.)

Because our memory verse for this series is perhaps the best loved and most quoted verse in the Bible, our lesson considers it in detail.

The *aim* of the lesson: To show that what God foretold was fulfilled when Christ was crucified.

What your students should *know*: Those who refuse to receive the Saviour are already condemned.

What your students should *feel*: A desire to have the gift of salvation.

What your students should *do*: Believe that God loves them and gave His Son for their sins. Place their trust in Him and receive His gift of everlasting life.

Lesson outline (for the teacher's and students' notebooks):

1. The brass serpent foretold Christ's crucifixion (John 3:1-14).
2. Believing in Christ gives everlasting life (John 3:15-16).
3. Rejecting Christ means separation from God forever (John 3:18).
4. Because of His love, Jesus died for the sins of the world (John 3:16).

The verse to be memorized:

For God so loved the world, that He gave His only begotten Son, that whosoever believeth in Him should not perish, but have everlasting life. (John 3:16)

THE LESSON

Show Illustration #12

The Lord Jesus was dead. His body was lying in a tomb sealed with a great stone. His disciples were bewildered by His crucifixion. (See John 2:19-22; also Mark 9:31-32; Luke 9:43-45.) Two strangers–strangers to us, at least–had buried Jesus. Both men were Jews. Joseph, who owned a new tomb, secretly begged for the body of Jesus. Joseph had become a believer in the Lord Jesus but, because he was afraid of the Jews, did not let others know that he believed.

Nicodemus helped Joseph, bringing with him about 100 pounds of spices. These were used to prepare the body for burial. Nicodemus was a ruler of the Jews and a member of the most religious group in Jerusalem. Why had he come? Probably he, too, believed in Christ. What would have caused a Jewish leader like Nicodemus to become a believer? When had he spoken to the Lord Jesus?

1. THE BRASS SERPENT FORETOLD CHRIST'S CRUCIFIXION
John 3:1-14

It was almost three years before. Nicodemus had gone to the Lord Jesus at night to talk with Him alone. That night the Son of God said to Him, "If you want to see the Kingdom of God, you must be born again." Those had been strange words to Nicodemus. How could he, at his age, be born again?

To explain more fully, the Lord Jesus reminded Nicodemus of an event from Jewish history–something which Nicodemus knew well. Jesus said it this way: "As Moses lifted up the serpent in the wilderness, even so must the Son of man be lifted up."

Nicodemus knew the meaning of the first part of that sentence. Hundreds of years before, the Jewish people had been angry at God and had spoken against Him and against their leader, Moses. To teach them the awfulness of such sin, God sent fiery serpents which killed untold numbers of people. So terrified were the others that they begged Moses to ask God to forgive them and take away the serpents. So Moses prayed for the people. (See Numbers 21:5-9.)

Show Illustration #13

God answered that prayer by telling Moses to put a brass serpent on a pole. "Everyone who is bitten," God said, "should look at the serpent of brass. If he does so, he will live." And that is exactly the way it was. This, Nicodemus understood. But what was the complete sentence? "As Moses lifted up the serpent in the wilderness, *even so must the Son of man be lifted up.*" Nicodemus may not have understood what the Lord Jesus meant the night He spoke those words. But when he stood at Calvary and saw Jesus hanging on the cross, he knew perfectly what Jesus had meant. For there, before his eyes, the One who had spoken to him was lifted up, just as the serpent of brass had been lifted up.

The Bible does not say exactly when Nicodemus was born into the family of God. But at some time he must have believed that the Lord Jesus Christ was the Son of God and received Him as Saviour. (One other time Nicodemus is mentioned. At that time, he defended Jesus. See John 7:40-52.)

2. BELIEVING IN CHRIST GIVES EVERLASTING LIFE
John 3:15-16

The record of Nicodemus' coming to the Lord Jesus is in John 3. Let us see what else is in that same chapter. The 16th verse which we have been memorizing says: "For God so loved the world, that He gave His only begotten Son, that whosoever believeth in Him should not perish, but have everlasting life."

Let us look at each part of this verse.

God so loved the world that He gave. This means that God is not an angry Judge waiting to destroy sinners. God is love. And before the earth was formed (1 Peter 1:20) God purposed to send His Son to earth. He would live a perfect life. But one day, taking upon Himself all the sin of the whole world, He would die as the substitute sacrifice. (See Isaiah 53:6; Romans 5:8; 1 Peter 2:24; 1 John 4:10.) He, the perfect One, would die in the place of every sinner. This was all in the plan of God. God loved the world so much that He gave His Son–gave Him to die.

God so loved the world that He gave *His only begotten Son*–His unique Son–that *whosoever believeth* in Him should not perish. "Whosoever" is a word that includes everyone. No matter how young you may be, or how old, no matter how sinful you are (and absolutely everyone has sinned), the "whosoever" includes you. God loves you and gave His Son for *you!*

And what is the "whosoever" to do? He is to *believe.* God loved, God gave–that whosoever *believeth.* What is it to believe? It is to place all your trust in the Lord Jesus Christ, to commit yourself and your affairs to Him. God says, "You cannot save yourself. But I have given My Son to die for you. Trust in Him. Whosoever believes in Him will not perish, but have everlasting life."

Show Illustration #14

What could be more simple than believing? One of the thieves who hung alongside the Lord Jesus prayed, "Lord, remember me when You come into Your Kingdom." This thief was so wicked that he himself said he deserved to die. (See Luke 23:40-43.) With nails holding him securely to his cross, there was nothing he could do to have his sins forgiven. Nothing, that is, except *to believe* that the Lord Jesus is the Son of God and to look to Him just as the sinners long before had looked at the serpent of brass. The One who sees the heart must have seen true belief in that thief, for He said, "Today you will be with Me in Paradise. This is a solemn promise."

"Whosoever believeth in Him should not perish but have *everlasting life.*" Everlasting life does not begin someday in the future after a person dies. It begins the moment one believes in the Lord Jesus. It is glorious to have life throughout all eternity. But everlasting life is more than that. It is the very life of God within you so you can have His life every day you are here on earth. God loved . . . God gave . . . you believe . . . and you have everlasting life.

The verse that follows our memory verse says: "For God sent not His Son into the world to condemn the world; but that the world through Him might be saved." Saving the world was more important to the Lord Jesus than life itself. He died so no one would need to be separated from God. He Himself showed the terror of being separated from God when He cried from the cross, "My God, My God, why have You forsaken Me?" Nothing could be worse than separation from God. Because God knows this He wants everyone in the world to be saved by believing in His Son. This is what the one thief did.

3. REJECTING CHRIST MEANS SEPARATION FROM GOD FOREVER
John 3:18

Show Illustration #15

But what about the other thief who was crucified? He ridiculed Jesus, shouting, "If You are the Promised One of God, prove it by saving Yourself–and us, too!" He would be forever separated from God. How do we know? We read in John 3:18, "He who believes on Him [God the Son] is not condemned: but he who believes not is condemned already, because he has not believed in the name of the only begotten Son of God."

The two men hanging on either side of Jesus were both sinners. Both deserved to die. One believed in the Lord Jesus, trusted Him, committed himself to Him. He was forgiven and given assurance of being with the Lord Jesus. The other scorned Jesus. He did not believe in Him. And because he did not believe in the Son of God, he could expect no pardon for sin. So he perished in everlasting darkness, forever separated from God.

4. BECAUSE OF HIS LOVE, JESUS DIED FOR THE SINS OF THE WORLD
John 3:16

Show Illustration #16

There were three crosses on the hill of Calvary. Two held thieves. On the central cross hung the perfect Son of God. For those who treated Him savagely, He prayed, "Father, forgive these people, for they do not know what they are doing." That is love, true love. God loved the world. He gave His Son. The Son loves you. He gave Himself for you. This verse you have memorized. It is written in your notebook.

Now make this chart in your notebook. According to John 3:18 there are:

> **TWO CLASSES OF PEOPLE** (John 3:18)
> #1 Condemned people–Those who do *not* believe in the Son of God.
> #2 People not condemned–Those who *do* believe in the Son of God.

When the Lord Jesus died 2,000 years ago, He took all your sin–even the vilest sin–upon Himself. As far as God is concerned, the problem of your sin is settled. What you must do now is settle the question of His Son. Do you believe Him to be the Son of God? Do you believe He died for your sins? Have you received Him as your own Saviour? If you have, you are not condemned. If you have not believed in Him, you are this very day condemned–that is, declared guilty. You do not wait until the day of judgment after death to find that out. You are condemned now. Why? Because you have heard of God's Son and His loving sacrifice which paid the penalty of your sins, and you have not believed in Him. Hear again what the Lord Jesus said, "He that believes not is condemned already *because he has not believed in the name of the only begotten Son of God.*" So, if you are condemned, it is because you have refused to receive the Saviour whom God has provided.

If I were to offer you a gift and you refused to take it, would the gift be yours? No! Jesus has offered you the gift of salvation. If you refuse to take it, it is not yours. And by refusing Him, you commit the worst of all sins–the sin God will not forgive.

God loves you; He gave His Son for you; if *you* believe in Him, *you* will not perish but *you* have (right now) everlasting life. Which are you: condemned? or not condemned?

www.ingramcontent.com/pod-product-compliance
Lightning Source LLC
Chambersburg PA
CBHW060805090426
42736CB00002B/168